GET LOST

around

ROBINSON CRUSOE ISLAND

GET LOST

around

ROBINSON CRUSOE ISLAND

by
Lee Miller

Lost Adventurer Books
ISBN: 9798664104684

For those that are terrified to wander from the path, but must.

June 23, 2020
Boston, Massachusetts (USA)

Foreward

I believe we become what we think about.

When my routine stumbled in 2020, my thoughts wandered and then raged. At first, this rage was directed at others, but then it turned inward. I had become a golden retriever wagging my way through a mindless life of treats and fuzzy blankets. Unable to run away, I ran towards my most sacred of places, books. My thoughts began waking me at 4am, directing me towards stories of explorers, round-the-world sailors, and treasure hunters. Wandering in a time of global lockdown was liberating. As I got to know these adventurers, what I found most compelling was that if you gave them a billion dollars, their tomorrow would be very much like their yesterday. These were people worth learning about.

Amidst the people were the places, and a small island off the coast of South America kept being mentioned. Slocum stopped there… to visit the lookout point of the man who spent 4 years alone there… where Spanish Revolution treasure was maybe buried… where the treasure was found… where the treasure was returned…where the Chilean government just (2019) issued a heavy equipment permit for excavating a UNESCO site. The past and current serendipity of it all fascinates me.

Hopefully this book gives you something to think about too.

<u>Satellite Images:</u>

front: Robinson Crusoe Island, Chile; NASA's Landsat 8, Jan. 12, 2014

Page 6: Más a Tierra, Chile; European Space Agency's Sentinel 2, Jan 3, 2020
Page 8: Fife, Scotland; NASA's Landsat 8, Oct. 2, 2019
Page 10: Kinsale, Ireland; NASA's Landsat 8, Oct. 16, 2019
Page 12: Santa Maria, Panama; NASA's Landsat 8, January 14, 2020
Page 14: Más a Tierra, Chile; NASA's Landsat 8, Jan. 12, 2014
Page 16: Más a Tierra, Chile; European Space Agency's Sentinel 2, June 6, 2020
Page 18: Más a Tierra, Chile; European Space Agency's Sentinel 2, Nov. 4, 2019
Page 20: Más a Tierra, Chile; NASA's Landsat 8, Dec. 3, 2016
Page 22: Más a Tierra, Chile; NASA's Landsat 8, Nov. 7, 2018
Page 24: Malpelo Island, Colombia; NASA's Landsat 8, March 9, 2020
Page 26: Más a Tierra, Chile; European Space Agency's Sentinel 2, Feb. 22, 2020
Page 28: Más a Tierra, Chile; NASA's Landsat 8, March 1, 2020
Page 30: Más a Tierra, Chile; European Space Agency's Sentinel 2, Nov. 4, 2019
Page 32: Más a Tierra, Chile; NASA's Landsat 8, March 17, 2014
Page 34: Más a Tierra, Chile; European Space Agency's Sentinel 2, March 23, 2020
Page 36: London, England; NASA's Landsat 8, Oct. 22, 2019
Page 38: London, England; European Space Agency's Sentinel 2, June 25, 2020
Page 40: Más a Tierra, Chile; NASA's Landsat 8, Dec. 11, 2013
Page 42: Gold Coast, Ghana; European Space Agency's Sentinel 2, May 8, 2020
Page 44: Más a Tierra, Chile; European Space Agency's Sentinel 2, June 6, 2020
Page 46: Valparaiso, Chile; European Space Agency's Sentinel 2, June 12, 2020
Page 48: Más Afuera, Chile; European Space Agency's Sentinel 2, May 25, 2020
Page 50: Robinson Crusoe Island, Chile; NASA's Landsat 8, Jan. 12, 2014

back: Robinson Crusoe Island, Chile; Euro. Space Agency's Sentinel 2, June 6, 2020

Más a Tierra

Juan Fernández Islands (Chile)

-33.62°N, -78.92°E

September 1704

After demanding to be marooned, Alexander was.

He was no longer cannon fodder, free from the continuously sinking worm-ridden hull and yellow fever that plagued its depths. Still, when backed by this deserted island, he cracked, swimming back to the boat and pleading for forgiveness. The captain laughed and sailed on.

The real Robinson Crusoe was born.

0   2.5   5 km
0   1.5   3 mi

Fife, Scotland

56.09°N, -3.04°E

1676-1703

Alexander Selcraig was born in 1676 on the north side of the Firth of Forth in Fife, Scotland.

The 7th son of a shoemaker, he seemed blessed with luck. With quick fists and a loud mouth, he spent almost 30 years brawling his way through days and nights. This luck seemed to have runout after he beat up his father, and the Catholic Church stepped in.

Yet just before Alexander's sentencing, he convinced Captain William Dampier to take him on as a navigator for Dampier's next privateering trip to South America, and away he went.

0   10   20 Km

Kinsale, Ireland

51.70°N, -8.51°E

1703

Privateers were pirates.

Pirating was a business. Essentials like gunpowder and swords, maintenance, and the payouts to crew were all wrapped within a constant balance of risk vs. reward, retreat vs. attack.

Flags defined a boat as friend or foe.

In this case, Knight Bachelor Thomas Escourt provided the British flag for the *St. George* and *Cinque Ports*, as well as the *request* (meaning the financing and blanketing security of all British ships) to raid the coast of South America, attacking mining villages and plundering Spanish ships. This business agreement also stipulated that until the total profit eclipsed £60,000 ($12M today), the privateers were not to return.

If necessary, Dampier and his crew would continue on, around Cape Horn and on to the gold mining villages near Lima, Peru and even Mexico if necessary. This numbers game even extended to the crew. The *St. George* and *Cinque Ports* left Kinsdale in September 1703 with 5-times as many men as they could comfortably accommodate.

Not everyone was not going to feel gold in their pocket.

10   20 km
5   10 mi

Santa María

Gulf of Panama
9.17°N, -79.77°E
1703

Problems were mounting only a few months in.

The drudgery of sleeping on mildewed bedding in wet clothes had lost its golden gleam. Their diet of biscuits, salted meat, and dried peas was starting to cause the swollen gums and purplish bruises of scurvy, and combined with yellow fever, was starting to kill the crew. By December 1703, the meat and grain was infused with roaches and rat droppings, but these were all smaller problem.

The big problem was that *St. George* and *Cinque Ports* were capturing treasure but they weren't keeping it.

Captain Dampier claimed he was keeping his hold open for a large quantity of gold, and with each successive raid, the crew was increasingly mutinous.

The gold rich region of Santa Maria on the Gulf of Panama (now Panama City and the Panama Canal) sounded like one giant treasure chest, with rumored stacks of gold bars everywhere. When they attacked this inland village, they were dumbfounded to find that a large forced defended the area. Quickly overwhelmed, they retreated to their boat and raced to the horizon.

0   10   20 km
0   5   10 mi

Más a Tierra

Juan Fernández Islands (Chile)
-33.62°N, -78.92°E
1704

Sick and defeated, with tired war-torn boats, in February 1704 both boats sailed to a small island 400 miles (650km) off the coast of Chile to resupply.

Soon after moving some of their gear and sails to shore for repair, a French boat appeared on the horizon, so they went on the attack.

The new plant was to return to the Bay of Panama, take what they could, divide the treasure, and then the *St. George* and *Cinque Ports* would go their separate ways.

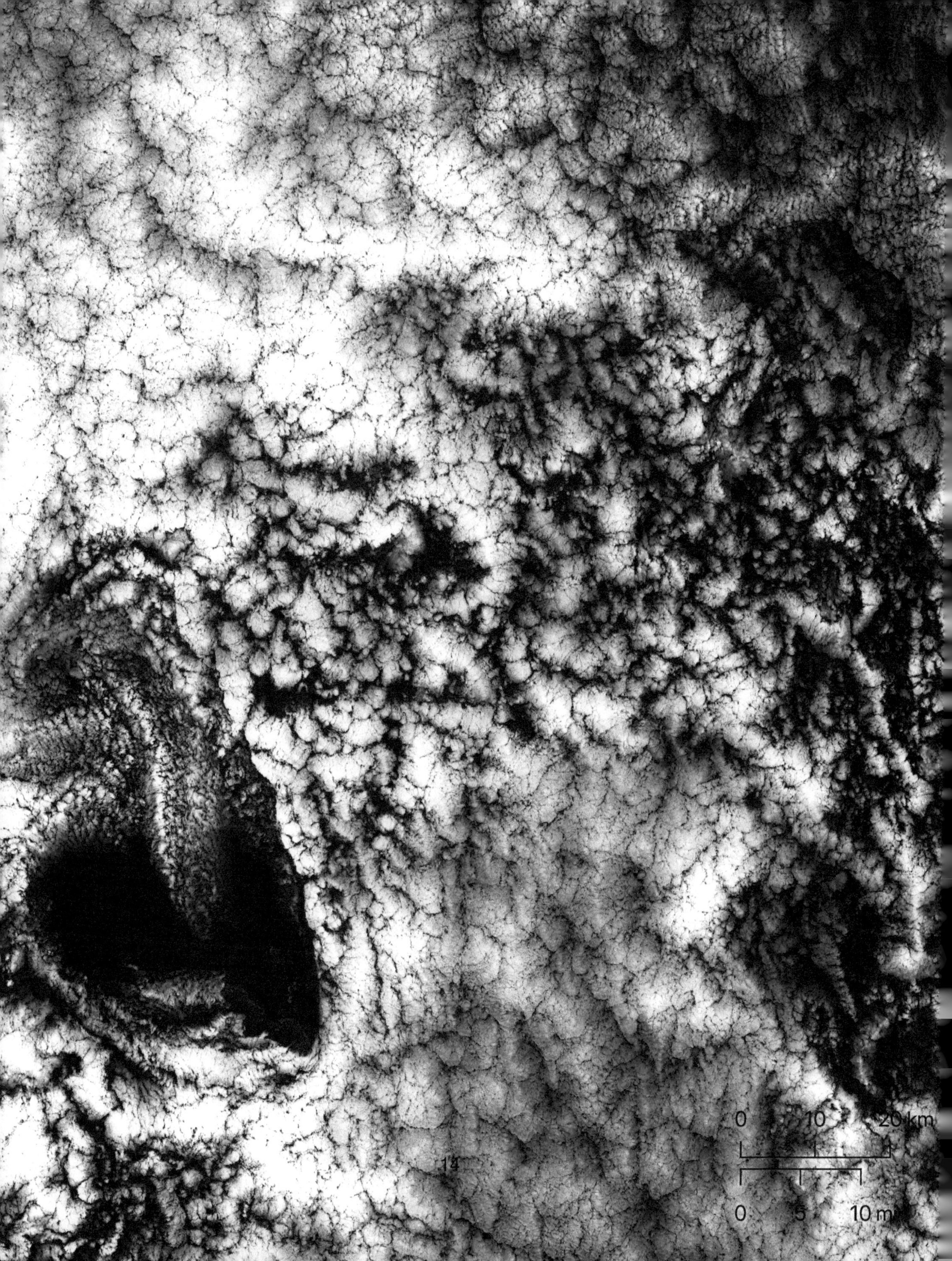
0   10   20 km
0   5   10 m

Más a Tierra

Juan Fernández Islands (Chile)

-33.62°N, -78.92°E

1704

By September 1704, *Cinque Ports* was on its own.

The hull was so damaged by worms and cannonballs that the bilge required non-stop pumping. They returned to Más a Tierra but the sails and gear from a few months before was gone. Still, the island's lobster, turnips, goats, and water provided a physical boost to the crew, but little was done to fix the *Cinque Ports*.

Alexander Selcraig, now known as Alexander Selkirk, thought this was a major oversight, as the masts, floors, and hull wouldn't survive the next storm or battle. Selkirk (expecting support from the crew) demanded that if the boat wasn't fixed, he would rather be put ashore.

He was.

Selkirk swam back to the boat, pleading for forgiveness, but the captain refused and pointed the boat towards the horizon. Selkirk's share of the their plunder was a Bible, bedding, hatchet, knife, his navigation tools, a pot, two pounds of tobacco, gunpowder, a musket and pistol, some cheese and jam, and a flask of rum.

0 5 10 km
0 2.5 5 mi

Más a Tierra

Juan Fernández Islands (Chile)

-33.62°N, -78.92°E

1704

Suicide framed Selkirk's thoughts the first few months. [1,2]

Southern Elephant Seals (*Mirounga leonine*), with their 2 ton 19 foot bodies dominated the beaches. Yet it wasn't their physical size, but their deep wailing sound "…too terrible to be made for human Ears," [1] that drove Selkirk to the edge of sanity, and away from the beach into the darker reaches of the jungle.

Inland, rats ruled, tirelessly biting and attacking Selkirk's toes and fingers through the night. The coarse volcanic rocky soil also tore at Selkirk's bare feet at every step, forcing him to stay where he was.

1. Steele, Richard (playwright and essayist) interviewed Selkirk in 1711, and his article in *The Englishman* made Selkirk famous
2. Rogers, Woodes (boat captain) *A Cruising Voyage Round the World: First to the South-Sea, Thence to the East-Indies, and Homewards by the Cape of Good Hope* (1712)

Más a Tierra

Juan Fernández Islands (Chile)

-33.62°N, -78.92°E

As Selkirk grew accustomed to the island, it became one giant feast.

Huge spiny lobsters (a clawless crayfish), were everywhere and easy to catch[1]. Goats were rampant but spry, and became not only a source of meat and milk, but also entertainment as his feet hardened against the constant rocky abrasions, and he learned to comfortably outrun them and throw them to the ground. Black pigment pepper provided some spice as well as fire starting material with a glancing blow from his musket flints. Freshwater was easy to find, as the steep volcanic slopes forced the clouds to rise and dump their water into numerous jungle streams.

Soon Selkirk was making an enchanting stew from the meats, valleys of watercress, cabbage palm, turnips, and a sprinkling of pepper.

Befriended feral cats now kept the biting rats away.

He clothed himself in goat skins, using the tanning skills taught to him by his shoemake father.

1. Fishing for, and the export of, these spiny lobsters is still the main source of income for about half of today's ~800 residents

0   10   20 km
0   5   10 mi

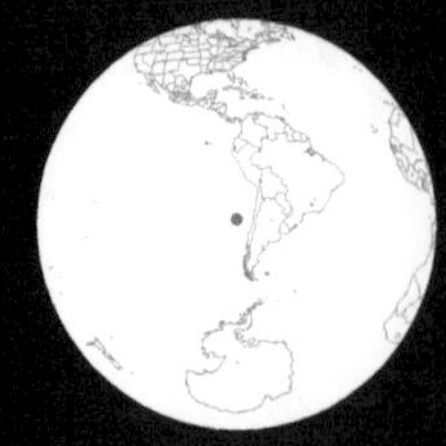

Más a Tierra

Juan Fernández Islands (Chile)

-33.62°N, -78.92°E

"…after the space of eighteen months, he grew thoroughly reconciled to his condition. When he made his conquest, the vigour of his health, disengagement from the world, the constant cheerful serene sky, and a temperate air, made his life one continual feast, and his being much more joyful than it had been before irksome. He [was] now taking delight in every thing."

1. Steele, Richard, <u>article</u> in *The Englishman* (1714), p.170,

0	5	10 km
0	2.5	5 mi

Malpelo Island

Colombia

3.99°N, -81.60°E

Caught in a storm off the coast of Barbacour, Colombia, *Cinque Ports* ran aground on Malpelo Island and sank.

The captain and 6 crew members survived, but after being rescued, spent the next 4 years in a Lima prison. [1]

1. Rogers, Woodes, p.145, *A Cruising Voyage Round the World: First to the South-Sea, Thence to the East-Indies, and Homewards by the Cape of Good Hope* (1712)

[tiny barren island to the right]

Más a Tierra

Juan Fernández Islands (Chile)
-33.62°N, -78.92°E

Selkirk spent several hours a day near the top of a mountain 300 meters above his camp on Cumberland Bay watching for ships. This lookout[1,2] allowed him to gaze for miles in every direction, giving him hours of notice before a landing party's arrival. Yet if he signaled an enemy ship, his fire would draw his enemies right to him.

1. memorialized with a bronze tablet on 'Selkirk's Lookout' by the crew of the HMS Topaze in 1869
2. visited by Joshua Slocum, described in *Sailing Alone Around the World* (1900)

5
10 m
25
0
2
mi

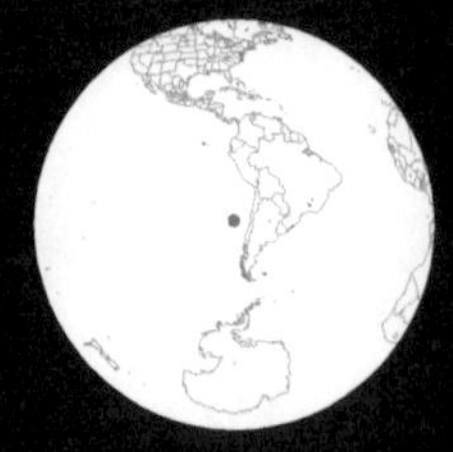

Más a Tierra

Juan Fernández Islands (Chile)

-33.62°N, -78.92°E

A Spanish ship arrived.

The pirates shot at Selkirk and chased him through the forest, but he was in incredible shape and knew his backyard well. Yet they did get close. When they paused during the pursuit to relieve themselves on a tree, Selkirk was perched directly above them [1].

If they had caught him, Selkirk would have been killed on the spot or turned into a slave in a South American gold mine.

1. Rogers, Woodes, *A Cruising Voyage Round the World: First to the South-Sea, Thence to the East-Indies, and Homewards by the Cape of Good Hope* (1712)

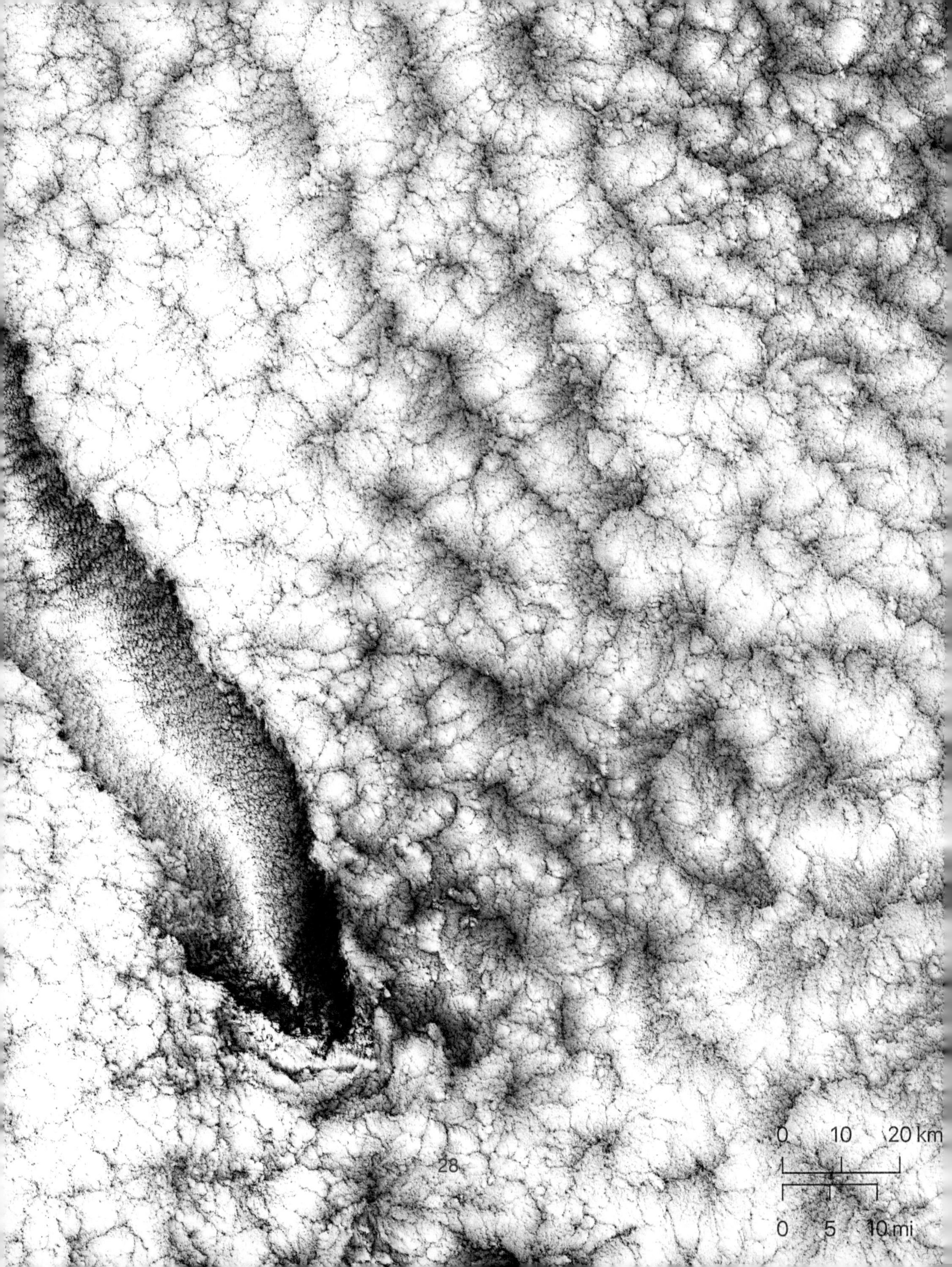
0 10 20 km
0 5 10 mi
28

Más a Tierra

Juan Fernández Islands (Chile)
-33.62°N, -78.92°E

Another Spanish ship arrived.

Selkirk remained hidden.

2.5
5 km
30
1.5
3 mi

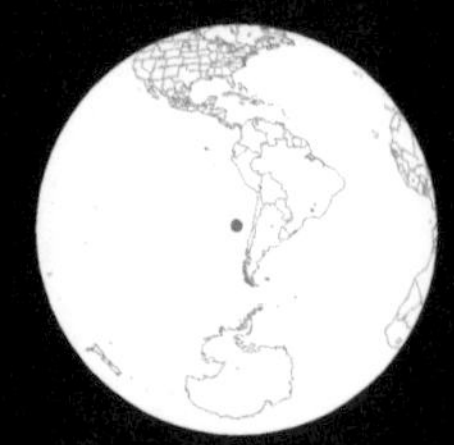

Más a Tierra

Juan Fernández Islands (Chile)

-33.62°N, -78.92°E

The *Duke* and *Duchess* arrived in Cumberland Bay. That night, judging the boats to be British, Selkirk started a signal fire that unsettled the crew. The next morning, an armed landing party went ashore but didn't return quickly as planned. Fearing hidden Spaniards had captured the shore party, they raised a French flag and sounded an alarm. When the crew returned, they "*…brought [back an] abundance of crawfish, with a man cloth'd in goat-skins, who looked wilder than the first owners of them*" p.125 [1].

Selkirk had been on the island for 4 years and 4 months.

Captain Rogers' navigator William Dampier [2] recognized Selkirk, easing tensions greatly. "*At his first coming on board [with] us, he had so much forgot his language for want of use, that we could scarce understand him, for he seem'd to speak his words in halves*" p.129. Selkirk recognized the crew's failing health, and through broken words and gestures, several crew members returned with him to the island in search of food. "*We had a bull-dog, which we sent with several of our nimblest runners, to help him in catching goats; but he distanc'd and tir'd both the dog and the men, catch'd the goats, and brought'em to us on his back*" p.127 [1]. Selkirk also helped the crew harvest a "*…store of turnip-greens, and water cresses in the brooks, which mightily refresh'd our men, and cleans'd'em from the scurvy*" p.135 [1].

"*By this one may see that solitude and retirement from the world is not such an insufferable state of life as most men imagine, especially when people are fairly call'd or thrown into it unavoidably, as this man [Selkirk] was…*" p.130 [1].

1. Rogers, Woodes, *A Cruising Voyage Round the World: First to the South-Sea, Thence to the East-Indies, and Homewards by the Cape of Good Hope* (1712)
2. Dampier was previously captain of the *St. George*, which had accompanied the *Cinque Ports* with Selkirk throughout South America

5 10 km
3 6 mi

Más a Tierra

Juan Fernández Islands (Chile)
~33.62°N, ~78.92°E

After 12 days of gorging themselves on fresh food, and replenishing the ships with wood, water, seal oil, vegetables, and salted mets, they left.

Alexander Selkirk, now shaved and clothed in linens, was made a navigator for Captain Rogers. Selkirk's speaking ability was returning,, though his feet kept swelling painfully in the confines of shoes, and the salted meats and breads were hard on his stomach.

Selkirk was also changing. Captain Rogers noted, *"It may likewise instruct us, how much a plain and temperate way of living conduces to the Health of the Body and the Vigor of the Mind, both which we are apt to destroy by Excess and Plenty, especially of strong Liquor, and the Variety as well as the Nature of our Meat and Drink: for this Man, when he came to our ordinary Method of Diet and Life, to he was sober enough, lost much of his Strength and Agility. But I must quit these Reflections, which are more proper for a Philosopher and Divine than a Mariner, and return to my own Subject."*

Duke and *Dutchess* had immense success over the next two years plundering their way along the coasts of Peru and Ecuador (Dutch East Indies at the time), only returning to London two years later.

Selkirk had been gone 8 years.

1.   Rogers, Woodes, (1712) *A Cruising Voyage Round the World*, p.130

0 2.5 5 km
34
16 3 mi

London

United Kingdom
51.51°N, 0.00°E
1712

Thanks to an article by Richard Steele in *The Englishman*, Alexander Selkirk was now famous. Food and drink flowed from any pub for the quick turn of one of his stories. Selkirk was also rich from his pirating on *Duke*, likely married two women, and spent most of his time wandering the pubs of Bristol and London.

Yet part of the marooned Selkirk from Más a Tierra remained. Behind his father's house in Lower Largo, Selkirk built a cave-like shelter where he would spend hours gazing upon the harbor.

Richard Steele ran into Selkirk a few months after their initial meeting, and much like Captain Rogers. noticed that Selkirk was changing quickly. The last paragraph of his article seemed even more true.

"This plain Man's Story is a memorable Example, that he is happiest who confines his Wants to natural Necessities; and he that goes further in his Desires, increases his Wants in Proportion to his Acquisitions; or to use his own Expression, 'I am now worth 800 pounds [1]*, but shall never be so happy, as when I was not worth a Farthing."* [2]

1. 800 pounds = $180,000 in 2020
2. Steele, Richard, article in *The Englishman* (1712), p.173,

0 10 20 km
36
0 5 10 mi

London

Daniel Defoe, an English trader, writer, and political activist was intrigued by Selkirk's story.

While it is not known if Defoe met with Selkirk directly, Defoe did meet with Captain Rogers (who rescued Selkirk) several times.

Robinson Crusoe, a story of a shipwrecked man who clothes himself in goatskins and eventually finds contentment on a small island, is now second only to the Bible in its number of translations.

20 km
5 10 mi

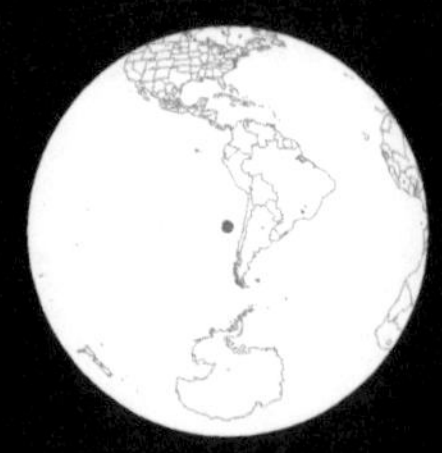

Más a Tierra

Juan Fernández Islands (Chile)
-33.62°N, -78.92°E

Back on Más a Tierra, something changed as well.

A few years after Selkirk returned to England, British navy admiral Lord Anson captured Juan Esteban Ubilla y Echeverria off the coast of South America's Pacific Coast.

In the throes of a hurricane, Ubilla told a story. Never the end of the Spanish War of Succession, the Spanish Hapsburgs (ruling family at the time) were being overthrown, so they hired Ubilla to transport the royal treasure from Spain to a safe place in South America.

That safe place was Más a Tierra, and was rumored to include 800 barrels of gold and silver coins, gold statues, and a necklace that belonged to the wife of the last Incan emperor Atahualpa.

Ubilla died soon thereafter.

0   10   20 km
0   6   12 ml

Gold Coast

Ghana
5.76°N, -0.669°E
1721

After spending 2 years in a Bristol (UK) jail for assault, Selkirk went back to sea as first mate on the naval warship HMS *Weymouth* to patrol for pirates off Africa's Gold Coast (now Ghana).

Riddled with yellow fever and possibly typhoid, 3-4 crew members a day were dying, and on a fair day with a light breeze from the north northwest, Alexander Selkirk died and was buried at sea.

0 5 10 km
0 3 6 mi

Más a Tierra

Juan Fernández Islands (Chile)
-33.62°N, -78.92°E
1761

Almost half a century after hearing of treasure on Más a Tierra, Britain's Lord Anson sent Captain Webb on *Unicorn* to recover it.

Webb and his crew recovered 864 bags of gold, 200 gold bars, 21 barrels of precious stones, and 60 chests of gold and silver coins. On their way home, the *Unicorn* encountered a violent storm, losing a mast and suffering serious damage. They returned to Más a Tierra, and buried the treasure in a new location.

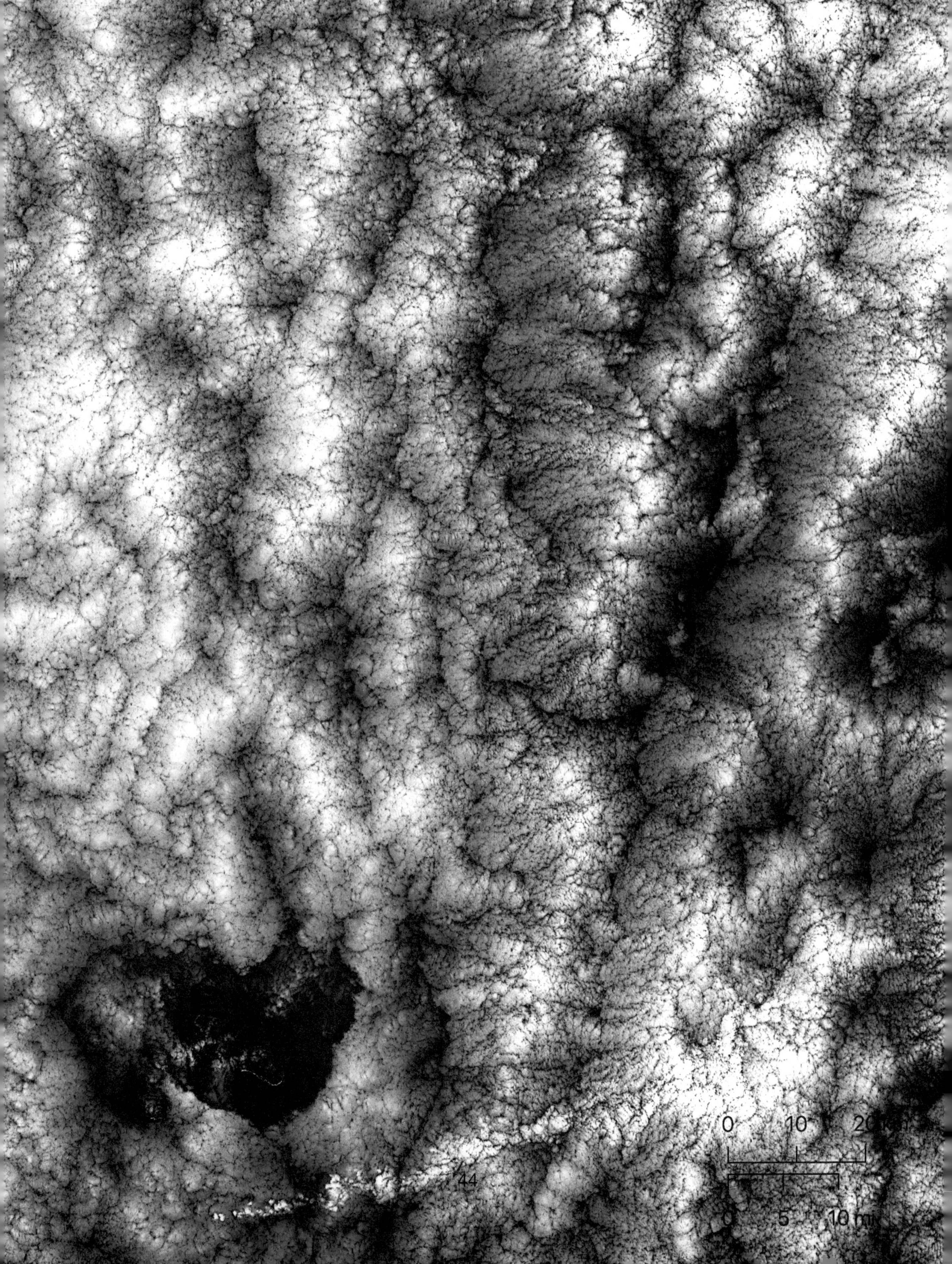

44
0   10   20 km
0   5   10 m

Valparaiso

Chile
-33.03°N, -71.61°E
1761

As the *Unicorn* limped its way back to the Chilean mainland 400 miles away, threats of mutiny grew rampant.

Becalmed a few miles off the coast, Captain Webb got into the small rowboat *Pinnance,* set fire to the *Unicorn,* and left the boat and all those onboard to burn.

46
0 5 10 km
0 3

Más Afuera

Juan Fernández Islands (Chile)
-33.79°N, -80.78°E
1966

In 1966, Chilean President Eduardo Frei Montalva changed the name of Más a Tierra to Robinson Crusoe Island and the nearby Más Afuera to Alejandro Selkirk Island. Located 100 nautical miles apart, it is unknown if Selkirk ever saw his future namesake.

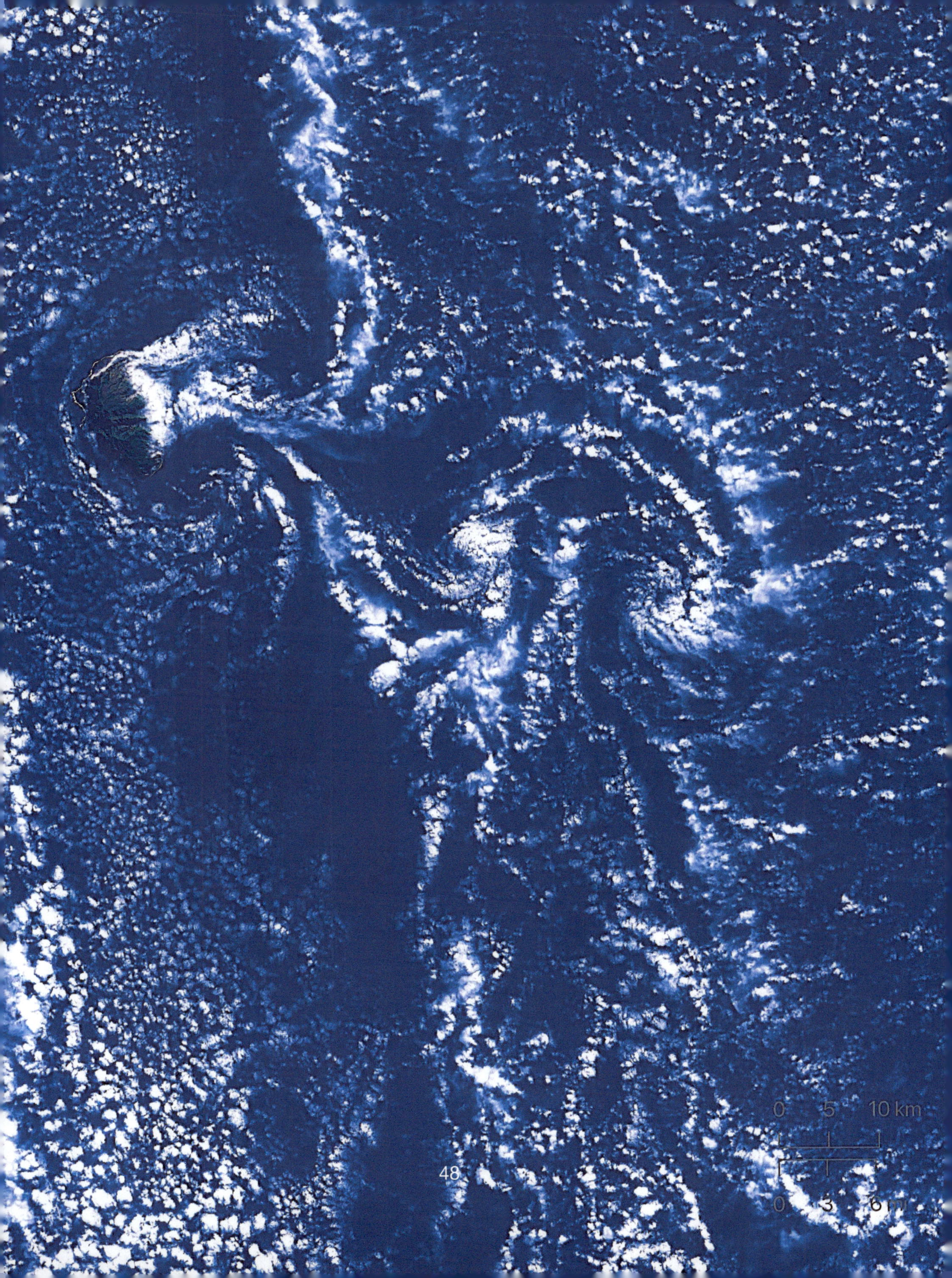

0 5 10 km
0 3 6

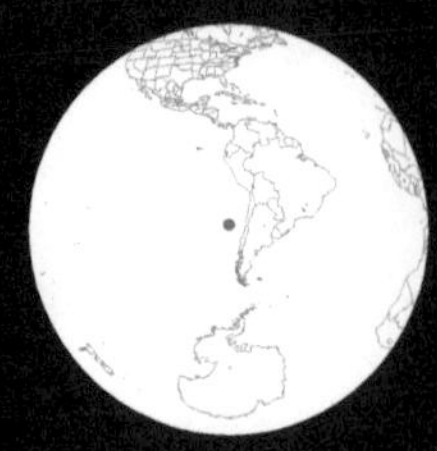

Robinson Crusoe Island

Juan Fernández Islands (Chile)
-33.62°N, -78.92°E
1998-

In 1998, businessman Bernard Keiser acquired a copy of Captain Webb's coded instructions from the family of Chilean politician Luis Cousiño.

Soon thereafter, Keiser began spending 8 months a year on the island, deciphering scratches on cave walls and decoding writing from English archives, and digging. Keiser is known to fund a men to dig six days a week for those 8 months each year. His search for the estimated $10 billion in treasure has now gone on for decades.

Given that much of Robinson Crusoe Island is a UNESCO Biosphere Reserve, their traditional tools have been limited to shovels and machetes. That changed on September 2, 2019 when the Chilean government issued a permit to Keiser for the use of heavy equipment to excavate a 400 square meter plot near Puerto Inglés, just northwest of where Selkirk likely spent 4 years and 4 months.

Maybe when the global pandemic of 2020 ends and international travel restrictions ease, the search for treasure will begin again. In this case, maybe 'x' actually marks the spot.

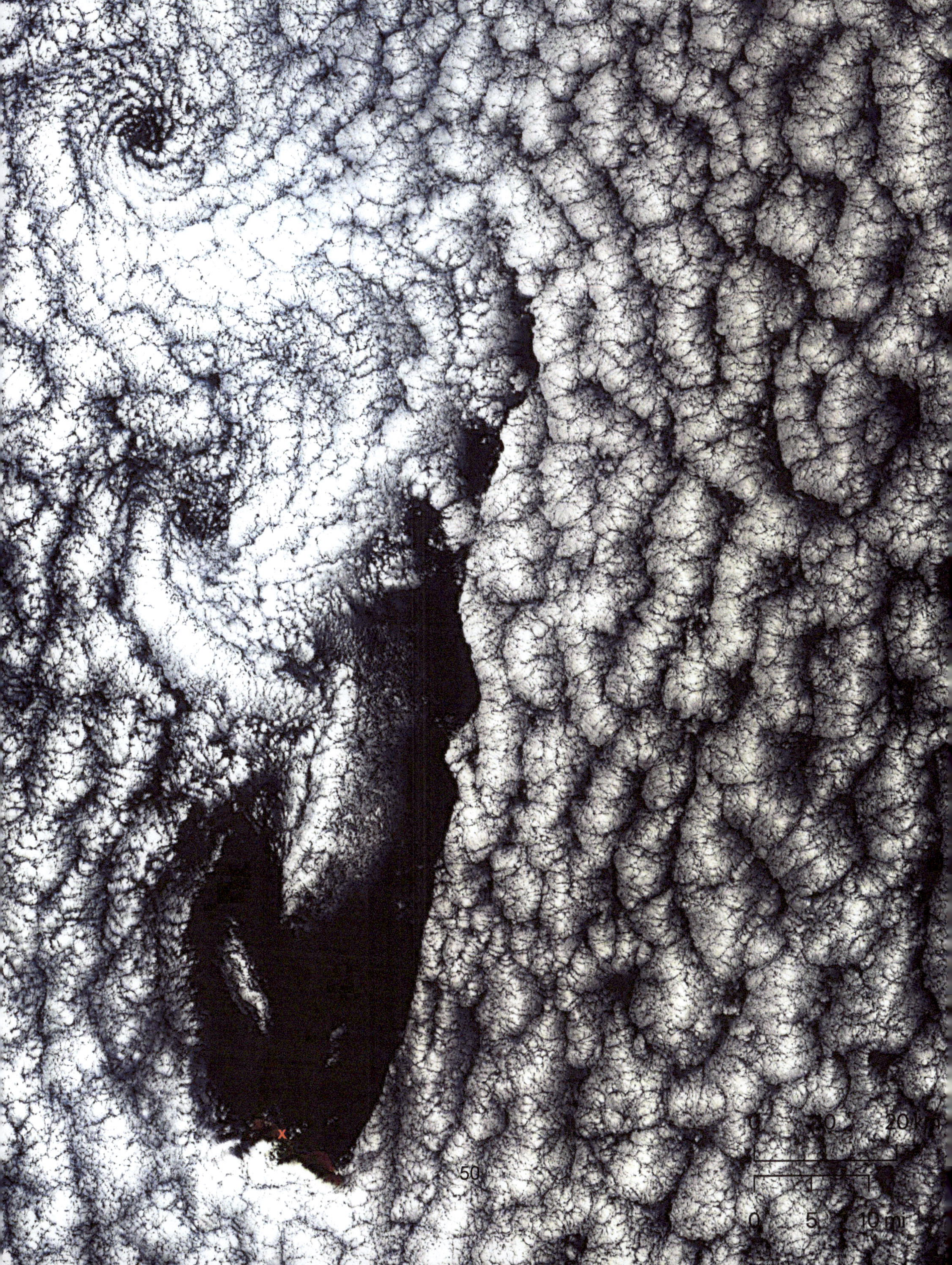
50
10
20
20
0   5   10 mi

The End

(for now)

If this story left you feeling motivated to do something
different from yesterday, Please consider….

- being nicer to yourself
- calling someone you love, telling them, and listen
- getting outside and be

If you want to tell me about it: lee.is.scared.too@gmail.com

This book was written in Boston during COVID-19 — Lee wanted to keep the adventure alive, even if all he could do was read and wonder.

Lee's early years wavered between conformity and revolt. After 3 failed college attempts, he drove west for a job fair at a ski resort. Twenty hours farther west than he'd ever been, he rounded a corner on Rt. 80 and saw the Rocky Mountains for the first time. Parked along the road watching the peaks sparkle in the morning sun, he wondered: *How would the world change if everyone had a glorious experience like this once in their life?*

Lee interviewed, but never followed up because *'what if I got the job?'* He returned to Pennsylvania, telling everyone he didn't get it.

Years later, he did get an internship in the deserts of Washington State, and purposefully drove through that same corner on Rt. 80. He had an incredible summer, but returned to the East Coast again.

Years later, you may have seen Lee on a wandering 6,000 mile road trip back to Washington. A 27' sailboat in John Wayne Marina became his home. He soloed mountains, surfed among dolphins, laughed with orcas, and bought a harley so he could buy a big boat. He trusted someone with his heart, which scared him more than anything before, but he didn't run. They spent 2 years rebuilding the big sailboat for crossing oceans, then sold it all and moved to Germany. A tech mogul bought and immediately sank *Lost Adventurer*.

Lee earned the PhD and postdoc at Max Planck in Germany, took a research fellowship at Harvard, and now works as a scientist.

It has been as easy and straightforward as it sounds.

Still married, and now with two young boys, Lee waits, dreams, and worries about how long is too long.